1 MONTH OF
FREE
READING

at
www.ForgottenBooks.com

By purchasing this book you are eligible for one month membership to ForgottenBooks.com, giving you unlimited access to our entire collection of over 1,000,000 titles via our web site and mobile apps.

To claim your free month visit:
www.forgottenbooks.com/free914985

ISBN 978-0-265-95419-5
PIBN 10914985

ANNUAL REPORT

OF

THE CURATOR

OF THE

MUSEUM OF COMPARATIVE ZOÖLOGY

AT HARVARD COLLEGE,

TO THE

PRESIDENT AND FELLOWS OF HARVARD COLLEGE,

FOR

1896-97.

CAMBRIDGE, U. S. A.:

UNIVERSITY PRESS: JOHN WILSON AND SON.

1897.

FACULTY OF THE MUSEUM.

Faculty.

CHARLES W. ELIOT, *President.*

ALEXANDER AGASSIZ, *Curator.*   GEORGE L. GOODALE.

—— ——, *Secretary.*   HENRY P. WALCOTT.

Officers.

ALEXANDER AGASSIZ . . . . . *Director and Curator.*
—— —— . . . . *Sturgis-Hooper Professor of Geology.*
NATHANIEL S. SHALER. . . . . *Professor of Geology.*
WILLIAM M. DAVIS . . . . . . *Professor of Physical Geography*
EDWARD L. MARK. . . . . . . *Hersey Professor of Anatomy.*
HENRY L. SMYTH . . . . *Assistant Professor of Mining.*

APPOINTED BY THE FACULTY OF THE MUSEUM.

WALTER FAXON. . . . . *Assistant in Charge.*
SAMUEL GARMAN . . . . *Assistant in Herpetology and Ichthyology.*
WILLIAM BREWSTER . . . . . *Assistant in Ornithology and Mammalogy.*
ALPHEUS HYATT . . . . *Assistant in Palæontology.*
SAMUEL HENSHAW . . . . . . *Assistant in Entomology.*
W. McM. WOODWORTH . . . . *Assistant in Charge of Vermes.*
ALFRED G. MAYER . . . . . . *Assistant in Charge of Radiates.*
C. R. EASTMAN. . . . . *Assistant in Vertebrate Palæontology.*
MISS F. M. SLACK . . . . . . *Librarian.*
MAGNUS WESTERGREN . . . . *Artist.*

APPOINTED BY THE PRESIDENT AND FELLOWS.

R. T. JACKSON . . . . *Instructor in Palæontology.*
C. B. DAVENPORT . . . . . . *Instructor in Zoölogy.*
G. H. PARKER . . . . *Instructor in Zoölogy.*
W. E. CASTLE . . . . *Instructor in Anatomy and Embryology.*
R. DeC. WARD . . . . *Instructor in Climatology.*
T. A. JAGGAR, JR. . . . . . . *Instructor in Geology.*
R. J. FORSYTHE . . . . *Instructor in Metallurgy.*
J. B. WOODWORTH . . . . . . *Instructor in Geology.*

F. C. WAITE . . . . *Assistant in the Zoölogical Laboratories.*
S. R. WILLIAMS . . . . *Assistant in the Zoölogical Laboratories.*
R. W. HALL . . . . *Assistant in the Zoölogical Laboratories.*
G. C. CURTIS . . . . *Assistant in the Geographical Laboratory.*
J. E. WOODMAN . . . . *Assistant in Geology.*
J. M. BOUTWELL . . . . *Assistant in Physical Geography.*
C. H. WHITE . . . . *Assistant in the Geological Laboratories.*

REPORT.

To the President and Fellows of Harvard College : —

During the past year the usual courses of instruction have been given at the Museum in the Natural History Laboratories. Those in Zoölogy were given by Professor Mark, and Doctors Davenport, Parker, and W. McM. Woodworth, assisted in the Laboratory work by Messrs. Henry R. Linville, John I. Hamaker, and J. H. Hathaway.

Professors Shaler and Davis, together with Instructors Robert Tracy Jackson, R. DeCourcey Ward, T. A. Jaggar, Jr., and J. B. Woodworth, gave courses of instruction in Geology, Palæontology, Physical Geography, and Meteorology. The Assistants in these departments were Messrs. Vernon F. Marsters, J. E. Woodman, and George C. Curtis.

The courses in Petrography and in Mining Geology, and allied subjects, are now given in the Mineralogical Department. These courses are in charge of Professor Wolff and Professor H. L. Smyth.

For the details of these courses of instruction, as well as of the summer courses in Geology, I would refer to the accompanying special reports of the Professors and Instructors.

I would specially call attention to the report of Professor Davis on the results of the teaching of Physical Geography during the summer courses.

The Newport Marine Laboratory has, as usual, been open to advanced students in Zoölogy. Eleven students spent a part of their time in the Laboratory collecting material for their special investigations, which they will continue and prepare for publication in Professor Mark's Laboratory at the Museum. I regret that hereafter it will be impracticable for me to open the Newport Laboratory to the students of the Zoölogical Department, as has been done for the past twenty years. I have during that time accumulated a large amount of material relating to the Marine Fauna of Narragansett Bay, which should be prepared for publication. The available room of the Laboratory will be required by the special Assistants who will aid me in this work, so that some other arrangement must be made to provide the facilities formerly furnished at Newport.

The Museum will now have at its command, for the use of its Assistants or other persons, the two tables at the Laboratory of the United States Fish Commission at Wood's Hole, to which it is entitled as one of the subscribers to the fund to establish the Commission Laboratory at Wood's Hole. One of the Museum Assistants and one student were admitted this year by Commander Brice to the Laboratory of the United States Fish Commission. The income of the Virginia Barret Gibbs Scholarship was assigned according to the terms of the gift.

Professor Faxon reports that he has completed the arrangement of the collection of recent Mollusca, undertaken in 1893. The collection of dried shells is now easily accessible, and in a state of permanent safety. It is contained in over 1,700 large standard wooden trays, and the bottles of the alcoholic collection, independently of the larger specimens contained in copper cans, fill about 100 trays. This of course does not include the Faunal or Systematic series of mounted specimens in the Exhibition Rooms.

Messrs. Henshaw, Garman, and Brewster report that the collections in their care are in excellent condition. Mr. Henshaw has devoted his time to the rearrangement of certain parts of our entomological collection, and to assisting those persons who have had occasion to consult the collection. He has also prepared for exhibition a collection of Galls, which has been placed in the Botanical Section of the Museum. In his report will be found a list of the additions to the Entomological Department.

The Exhibition Rooms have remained much as they were at the time of the last Report. A few specimens have here and there been intercalated to supply deficiencies, and poor specimens have been eliminated or better mounted.

Dr. Woodworth has been making some experiments with a view to improving the exhibition of alcoholic specimens. It is hoped to begin with the Synoptic and Atlantic Rooms, and substitute more artistically mounted alcoholic specimens for those now on exhibition.

To Professor Hyatt and to Mr. William Brewster the Museum is indebted for the care of their respective departments. Dr. R. T. Jackson has made excellent progress in the selection of the Fossils intended for the Palæozoic Exhibition Room.

Dr. Eastman has continued in charge of the Vertebrate Palæontological Collection, which is now in excellent order ; he has devoted his time principally to the study and increase of the collection of Fossil Fishes, and has made several excursions to interesting localities on behalf of our collection.

Dr. Mayer has spent the greater part of the last six months in collecting material for the new edition of the North American Acalephs. More than thirty new species of Jellyfishes were collected at the Tortugas. In the early spring he spent some time at Newport and at Nahant to obtain those species which disappear with the early summer. He also visited the coast of Maine to collect the more northern forms. It will require at least two years to collect the more common species along our Atlantic coast, and an off-shore expedition from the Tortugas to Eastport will be needed, in addition to extended visits at other points of the Atlantic coast, before we can expect to bring together a fair representation of the Acalephan Fauna of our Atlantic coast. Dr. Mayer has also revised the labels of the alcoholic collection of Deep-Sea Corals, many of which had become faded.

Dr. Woodworth, who has been engaged in the revision of our collection of Worms, has undertaken to work up the Annelids of the Atlantic coast of the United States. The Museum is in possession of a large collection of colored drawings of species made by Professor Agassiz and his assistants, extending from the coast of Massachusetts to Florida. Of many of the species no specimens are extant, and it is hoped that some use may now be made of this valuable systematic material, which has been awaiting publication for so many years. During the past summer Dr. Woodworth has spent his time at the Newport Laboratory collecting the species of Narragansett Bay.

Collections have been sent in exchange to Professor Orton and to the Smithsonian Institution.

Specimens have been sent for examination to Mr. P. F. Kendall, to Mr. Gamble, to Dr. Thiele, and to Dr. Montgomery, who has prepared a report on the Gordiacea of the Museum Collection, together with the results of his preliminary examination on other collections of the group accessible to him.   His report will appear in one of the forthcoming Bulletins, and will be illustrated by 15 Plates.

Among the principal collections we have received I may mention a collection of Devonian fish remains from Professor S. Calvin, State Geologist of Iowa; a collection of Worms, kindly sent from Sydney by Dr. Collingwood; and a valuable invoice of South American Fishes and Reptiles, from Dr. Lataste. The large collection of Corals from the northern part of the Great Barrier Reef made for me by Professor H. A. Ward has safely arrived at the Museum.   This fine collection was made under considerable difficulties by Professor Ward, but to his perseverance and enthusiasm we owe one of the best possible representations of the species of reef builders of the northeast coast of Australia.   In due time the collection will be placed on exhibition in the Systematic Room of Polyps.

We have also received a valuable collection of North Atlantic Crustacea from Canon Norman.

The Museum is likewise indebted to Messrs. Dendy, Jameson, and Hallez, for valuable additions to our collection of Turbellaria, Planarians, and Nemerteans.

We have also received a valuable collection of Mammals and Birds from Borneo and the Celebes, presented to the Museum by Dr. W. H. Furness.

The additions to the Library by purchase, gift, and exchange have kept up with those of the preceding year.

The Library now numbers, including the Whitney Library, over 31,000 volumes, and about 2,000 pamphlets which are not yet arranged for binding.

For a complete list of the publications of the Museum during the past year I refer to Appendix A.   A list of the publications of the Officers and Instructors of the Museum other than those contained in our Memoirs and Bulletins will be found accompanying the special Reports.

Excellent progress is making with several of the Reports on the " Albatross " Expedition of 1891 since the last Report.   Mr. Westergren has been engaged upon the Plates of Mr. Garman's Monograph of the Fishes.

Professor Lütken reports that he has completed the examination of the Ophiurans.

Professor H. B. Ward has also completed his Report on the Sipunculids, and Dr. Hansen that on the Isopods.

The proofs of the Report on the Acalephs have been sent to Dr. Maas, and it is hoped that his Memoir will be issued shortly.

Of the " Blake " Reports, we have published the Memoir by Professors Milne-Edwards and Bouvier on the Galatheidæ (Vol. XIX. No. 12), and a Bulletin (Vol. XXX. No. 3), Supplementary Notes on Crustacea, by Professor Faxon.

The Monograph on the American Crinoidea Camerata by Wachsmuth and Springer, by far the most extensive publication we have yet undertaken, has been issued by the Museum as Volumes XX. and XXI. of the Memoirs, accompanied by an Atlas of 83 Plates. The Heliotype Printing Company of Boston deserves great credit for the thorough manner in which it fulfilled its contract for the delivery of the Plates, and we are greatly indebted to Mr. Westergren for his endless care in the supervision of the presswork of the Plates.

The Corporation has continued the allowance of $400 made in previous years to aid in the publication of some of the Contributions from the Zoölogical Laboratory.

Of the Bulletins we published two numbers of the Geological Series relating to the Florida Reefs, by myself, Mr. L. S. Griswold, and Dr. E. O. Hovey (Vol. XXVIII. Nos. 2 and 3). Volume XXX. of the Bulletin has also been issued, containing four numbers of Contributions from the Zoölogical Laboratory, in charge ot Professor Mark, and one number by Dr. Woodworth and myself on the Variations in the Genus Eucope.

Among the papers which are ready for the press I may mention the report of my Visit to the Great Barrier Reef, and short papers by Dr. Woodworth on the Planarians, and by Dr. Mayer and myself on some Acalephs of the Barrier Reef.

A short Memoir on the Genus Dactylometra, by Dr. Mayer and myself, is also ready for the printer.

This publication will probably be delayed until my return from the Fiji Islands, where I have planned to pass the greater part of next winter in studying the coral reefs of that group. I shall be accompanied by Dr. Woodworth and Dr. Mayer as assistants. The steamer "Yaralla" has been chartered in Sydney for the expedition, and she is to meet us at Suva late in October. The outfit for the expedition has been shipped to Sydney to be placed on board the steamer we have chartered. In addition to the usual apparatus, for photographic purposes, for sounding and dredging, and for pelagic work, we take a diamond drill outfit, and hope to find a suitable locality for boring on the rim of one of the atolls of the Fijis. The boring machinery will be in charge of an expert sent by the Sullivan Machine Company, from whom this machinery was obtained. The Directors of the Bache Fund have made a large grant towards the expenses of this boring experiment.

I am also indebted to Professor Brandt of Kiel for superintending for me the construction of a deep-sea self-closing townet, such as was used in the " National " Expedition. Dr. Richard, of Paris, sent me a modified Giesbrecht net, such as is used by the Prince of Monaco on the ": Princess Alice," and Dr. A. Dohrn kindly deputed Dr. Giesbrecht to send me one of the Giesbrecht nets from the Naples Station. These, together with the old and new styles of Tanner net, which we take with us, as well as a self-closing net adopted by Mr. Townsend of the " Albatross," which he was kind enough to have made for me, will give us the means of comparing these different styles of deep-sea townets, and of testing their comparative efficiency under similar circumstances.

Thanks to the kind offices of the State Department at Washington, we carry letters to the Governor of the Fijis from the Foreign Office in London.

I have to thank specially Admiral Wharton, R. N., Hydrographer of the Admiralty, for his assistance and counsel in regard to our visit to the islands, and also Captain W. O. Moore, R. N., for his kindness in placing at my disposal his experience and the information he acquired while surveying the Fijis. I must also mention the late Sir John B. Thurston, Governor General of the Fijis, who from the first conception of the expedition took the deepest interest in our success. We shall greatly miss his advice, and the knowledge he had gathered during the long period of his administration in that part of the South Sea Islands.

Mr. Theodore Lyman, one of the most efficient and devoted friends of the Museum, died at Nahant on the 9th of September, 1897. Withdrawn since 1885, by reason of failing health, from any active share in the affairs of the Museum, he nevertheless was and must ever remain identified with its history. The regret for his absence, always deeply felt by his colleagues, made a blank in their ranks which his death only accentuates. Not only did they value him for his personal acquirements, and for his sympathy with the general interests of the Museum, but also for his genial character, which brought with it a cordial, cheering influence appreciated by all his co-workers.

From his youth he was a favorite pupil of Professor Agassiz, and that relation, notwithstanding their difference of age, ripened into friendship with advancing years. He entered with zeal into all the plans of Professor Agassiz for the establisment of a Museum at Cambridge, and the creation of a school of Natural History at Harvard University. He was one of the original trustees of the Museum, and served as its Treasurer in addition to his work as Assistant in Zoölogy.

After the Charter of the Museum was transferred to the Corporation of Harvard University, he became a member of the Museum Faculty, and acted as its Secretary. In all these official positions his devotion to the founder of the Museum, his business capacity, his common sense and sound judgment, were of great value in raising the institution to its present position.

After the death of Professor Agassiz, Mr. Lyman continued his services to the Museum, until he became incapacitated for work by the disease which finally ended his life. His letter of resignation shows what it cost him to give up his scientific pursuits, and sever his connection with the institution to which he was so deeply attached. It signified also his full recognition of the ordeal he was called upon to face, and which he bore through years of suffering with invincible fortitude.

Mr. Lyman's scientific work was devoted to fisheries and to the study of Brittle Starfishes. As Fish Commissioner of Massachusetts he gave the State valuable service, and published a number of annual reports from 1866 to 1881.

His zoölogical work began with short papers on ornithological subjects; he subsequently became interested in corals, and finally devoted himself specially to Ophiurans. The first Illustrated Catalogue of the Museum was from his pen, and this important monograph on Ophiurans was followed by numerous papers on the same subject, treating of new species of the group. He wrote the Report on the Ophiurans of the "Hassler" Expedition, of the "Challenger," and of the "Blake" Reports, which include by far the larger number of species of Ophiurans dredged by those deep-sea exploring expeditions.

ALEXANDER AGASSIZ.

CAMBRIDGE, October 1, 1897.

REPORT ON THE COURSES OF INSTRUCTION IN GEOLOGY.

BY PROFESSOR SHALER.

DURING the Academic year 1896–97, the following named courses of instruction were given in the laboratories and in the field by the instructors of the Department of Geology and Geography. It will be noted that certain courses formerly enumerated in this list no longer appear, having been incorporated in the new Department of Mineralogy and Petrography.

Instruction in General Geology.

(Geol. 4.) A half-course in Elementary Geology: two lectures a week by N. S. Shaler, with required reading in Dana's Manual of Geology. Assisted by J. E. Woodman. Other instructors in the Department gave lectures on particular phases of geology. The course was attended by three hundred and twenty students.

(Geol. 5.) A half-course in Elementary Field and Laboratory Work, requiring two-hour exercises twice a week during the laboratory season, and one half-day a week in the field during the spring months. This course was given by Mr. J. B. Woodworth, assisted by J. E. Woodman. It was attended by seventy-seven students.

(Geol. 8.) A course in General Critical Geology, two lectures a week, by J. B. Woodworth, assisted by J. E. Woodman. Field work in the spring and autumn; required reading and library work in the winter; attended by eighteen students.

(Geol. 22a.) A course in Geological Field and Laboratory Work, designed to afford special training in methods of investigation, conducted by T. A. Jaggar, Jr., under the supervision of the instructors of the Department. Attended by six students.

(Geol. 22b.) A course in geological investigation, intended to lead to results worthy of publication; under the direction of the instructors of the Department. Attended by one student.

(Geol. 16.) A half-course in Glacial Geology, by J. B. Woodworth. Two hours a week with field work. Attended by seven students.

(Geol. 17.) A course in Experimental and Dynamical Geology, by T. A. Jaggar, Jr. Two lectures a week with laboratory work. Attended by two students.

Instruction in Physical Geography and Meteorology.

(Geol. 2.) A half-course in Physiography, by W. M. Davis, assisted by V. F. Marsters. Two or three lectures a week, with laboratory work and recitations, first half-year. Attended by fifty-three students.

(Geol. 1.) A half-course in Elementary Meteorology, by R. DeC. Ward. Two or three lectures a week, with laboratory work and recitations, second half-year. Attended by ninety-nine students.

(Geol. 3.) A half-course in Physiography and Meteorology, by W. M. Davis and R. DeC. Ward. Two lectures a week. Attended by thirteen students.

(Geol. 6.) A half-course in the Physiography of the United States, by W. M. Davis. Lectures, library work, and reports, second half-year. Attended by seventeen students.

(Geol. 19.) A half-course in Climatology, by R. DeC. Ward. Three lectures a week, first half-year. Attended by twelve students.

(Geol. 20.) A course in advanced Physiography, by W. M. Davis. Conferences held once a week. Attended by five students.

Instruction in Palæontology.

(Geol. 14.) A half-course in Palæontology, by N. S. Shaler, assisted by R. T. Jackson. Two lectures a week, with theses. This course was attended by seventeen students.

(Geol. 13.) A course in Invertebrate Palæontology, by R. T. Jackson. Two lectures a week, with laboratory work. Attended by two students. This course will be discontinued; its place to be filled by a similar proposed course in the Zoölogical Department.

(Geol. 15.) A course in Historical Geology, designed to train advanced students in the use of fossils in determining geological horizons, by N. S. Shaler and R. T. Jackson. This course was taken by three students.

Instruction in the Summer Schools.

(Geol. S. 1.) An elementary course in General Geology, given in Cambridge, by Professor Shaler and Dr. G. E. Ladd. This course was attended by nineteen students.

(Geol. S. 2.) A course in Geological Field Work, by N. S. Shaler and J. B. Woodworth. After a week spent in Cambridge, the class went into the field in Southern New England, under the guidance of Mr. Woodworth. Attended by three students.

19. (Geog. 1.) A course in Elementary Physiography, beginning July 3, and lasting six weeks, by W. M. Davis, assisted by W. H. Snyder and M. H. Wright. Lectures, laboratory work, and excursions. Attended by seventy-eight students.

20. (Geog. 2.) A course in the Physiography of the United States, beginning July 3, and lasting six weeks, by W. M. Davis, assisted by J. M. Boutwell. Lectures, reports, and theses. Attended by eleven students.

The instruction in Elementary Geology was given in two half-courses, one a lecture course by Professor Shaler, with occasional lectures by other members of the department. Mr. J. E. Wood-man acted as Assistant during the year. The remainder of the instruction in elementary geology was given in the form of a laboratory and field course by Mr. J. B. Woodworth, assisted by Mr. Woodman.

An advanced course in General Geology was given by Mr. Wood-worth as in former years. The same instructor repeated his half-course in glacial geology, having particular relation to the glacial deposits in the eastern half of the United States. Field work was maintained in both of these courses. Mr. Woodworth reports a number of specimens added to the teaching collection for geological students and the placing of a show case in the Laboratory for the reception of materials which have been described in publications by the officers of the Department. It is hoped thus to preserve the specimens which have been made the basis of important conclusions.

During the year, Professor Shaler and Mr. Woodworth continued the examination of the Richmond coal field in Virginia, the costs of the investigation being defrayed by the United States Government. Professor Shaler has completed a report on the Geology of Cape Cod for the United States Geological Survey.

During July and August Mr. Woodman visited Central Nova Scotia, making investigations relating to the suitability of the region for advanced geological teaching, and to the structure of the rocks, the origin of the gold-bearing veins and their contents, and the general mining policy of the Province.

In the Summer Schools of the University, two courses in Geology were given under the direction of Professor Shaler. The first

of these was an elementary course given in Cambridge, the immediate supervision of which in the laboratory and in the field was
placed in the hands of Dr. G. E. Ladd, of the Geological Survey of
Georgia, formerly an instructor in this Department. The second
school was given for five weeks in the field, the time being devoted
to an examination of the general geology of Southern New England.
A detailed itinerary of the route taken has been published in the
announcements of the Summer Schools for the year 1897. On
these journeys materials were collected for the teaching collection
of the Laboratory.

Specimens of fulgurite from the sand beach of Lighthouse Point,
Marquette, Mich., were presented by Mr. H. W. Kidder.

Dr. R. T. Jackson reports that the collections used in teaching
Palæontology are in good condition. Considerable additions have
been made to the series of enlarged photographic diagrams, of
which there are now eighty-five. Some excellent specimens of
Cambrian Trilobites from British Columbia were received from
Mr. F. N. Balch, of the Graduate School. A fine crinoid stem
from the Chemung of Pennsylvania was received from Mr. C. O.
Macfarlane, Superintendent, Long Valley Coal Co., Towanda, Pa.
A number of desirable specimens were received from Mr. J. B.
Woodworth, for all of which the Department records its thanks.

A good representation of the plants of the Dakota Group of
Kansas was purchased of Mr. C. H. Sternberg, of Lawrence,
Kansas. A number of fossils selected to fill gaps in the collection
were purchased of Prof. H. A. Ward, of Rochester.

The collection of Invertebrate Fossils is now a very good one,
embracing representative genera of all the groups which are preserved in the geological record. It includes many microscopic
slides and other preparations to elucidate structural detail. The
collection which illustrates Historical Geology is also satisfactory.
While there is need of additional material in many groups, there
is a considerable representation of fossils from every important
geological horizon from the Lower Cambrian to the Quaternary.

Dr. Jackson spent considerable time in working on the Palæontological Collections of the Museum.

Mr. T. A. Jaggar, Jr. reports as follows concerning the advanced
courses in geological field and laboratory work.

In Geology 22*a*, Messrs. Buckman and Kendall worked together on the stratigraphic relations of the sedimentary rocks about Hoppin Hill, near North Attleborough, Mass.

In Geology 17, Mr. V. F. Marsters, in collaboration with Mr. Jaggar, completed a preliminary series of experiments on the influence of rate of compression and initial fracture in deformation of strata. This half-course in experimental geology was given for the first time: a series of lectures extending throughout the first half-year reviewed the work of former experimenters, and systematic laboratory work covered experiments in deformation, delta deposition and sedimentation, ice motion, vortical motion of fluids and its geological work (ripple-mark, etc.), rock and mineral synthesis (including Moissan's experiment with the electric furnace). During the second half-year Mr. Marsters made a series of tests with various crucibles to determine the most effectual and inexpensive method of using the blast furnace for rock synthesis, and completed several syntheses of basalt.

The Gardner Collection of Photographs has been in the hands of a committee composed of Messrs. J. B. Woodworth, Ward, and Woodman.

A case has been provided for the reception of lantern slides, with a capacity of 3,500 slides. About one hundred slides have been added during the year, mainly reproduced from photographs already in the collection.

341 catalogued photographs have been added to the collection since the last Report, bringing the number up to 3,594. A few faded photographs have been condemned and thrown aside. The most notable additions during the year have been a number of views of the High Sierras taken by Mr. J. S. Solomons, of San Francisco; a set of Norwegian views selected by Dr. Hans Reusch, Director of the Geological Survey of Norway; a set of coastal views from Maine and Massachusetts, donated by Mr. John L. Gardner, Jr.; and a set acquired by purchase from the Iowa Geological Survey. Gifts were received from Mr. G. W. Griffith of a panorama of the Muir Glacier in Alaska, and from Mr. J. C. Clark of English views; also from Mr. J. H. Ropes, and from Mr. C. I. Wright.

REPORT ON COURSES IN PHYSICAL GEOGRAPHY.

By Professor W. M. Davis.

During the past year, the courses in Elementary and Advanced Physiography given by Professor Davis, and the course in Elementary Meteorology given by Mr. Ward, have been conducted on the plan described in recent reports. The course on Climatology by Mr. Ward in the first half-year was presented for the first time, and the course on the Physiography of the United States by Professor Davis in the second half-year was given for the second time after an interval of a year, in which a similar course was given on Europe. It is believed that the course on Climatology will prove to be a valuable addition to the preparation of those who later take up the study of medicine, as at present this important subject seldom finds adequate treatment in medical schools. The acceptance with which a series of four lectures on Climatology by Mr. Ward were received by an audience of physicians in Boston in the spring of 1897 gives further ground for this belief. The course on the United States was strengthened by a much more extended exhibition of reports and essays, bearing on the various divisions of the country than when it was given before : in this connection, Darton's Bibliography of American Geology (Bulletin 127, U. S. Geol. Survey) proved very serviceable.

Apart from the duties connected with courses of instruction, Mr. Ward undertook to inquire, by means of a circular letter addressed to medical schools, into the amount of attention given to Climatology in their regular course of study, with the result intimated above. In the latter part of the year, Mr. Ward gave much care to preparations for his voyage around South America, including visits to various ports, and a sojourn at the Harvard Observatory at Arequipa, Peru. He left New York on this voyage early in June, 1897, and will return to Cambridge in January, 1898. During the past year, Mr. Ward has prepared an Outline of

Requirements in Meteorology for the Committee on Admission Requirements, and has edited a series of " Current Notes on Meteorology " in Science. The chief additions to his laboratory collections are a series of Mercator wall maps of isotherms and isobars, enlarged from the maps in Buchan's Challenger Report for lecture use.

Ten years ago, a series of geographical models designed by Professor Davis was constructed with the aid of Mr. J. H. Emerton of Boston for use in one of the Lowell free lecture courses in the Teachers' School of Science of the Boston Society of Natural History. Several sets of these models, reproduced in paper by Mr. Emerton, were sold to colleges and schools. One set has been in constant use in the Geographical Laboratory of the Museum, and has been of great service ; but it has been increasingly desirable in recent years to make a new series of models of greater accuracy, and on an improved plan. Hitherto, this has been impossible on account of the expense involved in securing the services of a competent modeller ; but in the autumn of 1896, a fund of several hundred dollars was subscribed for this object by a number of ladies and gentlemen of Boston interested in educational problems, and a long cherished plan was put into execution. Among the subscribers to this fund, Miss Marian C. Jackson must be mentioned, as without her support the undertaking could not have reached its present measure of success. The services of Mr. George C. Curtis, recently a student of geology and geography in the Lawrence Scientific School, were secured in October, 1896, and in June, 1897, ten sets of three models each — or thirty models in all — had been constructed after original designs by Professor Davis : one model representing a deeply dissected mountainous region, descending to the sea ; the second, including a coastal plain revealed on the border of the mountains in consequence of a regional elevation ; the third exhibiting an irregular coast of promontories and bays, produced by a general depression of the first. An account of the models has been published in the Proceedings of the Boston Society of Natural History, and all the sets thus far constructed have been engaged by various Normal and other schools, although not at this date actually sold. It is hoped that it will be possible to continue this work during the coming year, with the double object of supplying schools with better materials for teaching geography, and inducing some enterprising publisher to undertake the duplication of such models in larger numbers and at low price. Eventually, it is desired to establish a Museum of Systematic Geography, in which an extended series of typical land forms shall be exhibited.

During the past year, Professor Davis has completed his long delayed Report on the Triassic Formation of Connecticut for the United States Geological Survey, and has made good advance in the preparation of a text book of Elementary Physiography. In connection with his service on the Committee on Admission Requirements, he has drawn up an Outline of Requirements in Physiography for the use of secondary schools. In order to extend the introduction of topographical maps in elementary teaching, he has written pamphlets on the use of the State Map in grammar schools, which have been published by the educational authorities in New York and Massachusetts, thus following the example set by Connecticut and Rhode Island a year ago. He has continued the editing of " Current Notes on Physiography " in Science, and with Mr. Ward has joined the board of associate editors of the Journal of School Geography, conducted by Professor R. E. Dodge, of the Teachers' College, New York City. In company with students, or alone, he has visited the Triassic region of Connecticut, the cuspate forelands of Narragansett Bay and Nantucket, and the peculiar coastal plain of Southern Maine. Late in June, he addressed the University Convocation at Albany, N. Y., on the Present Trend of Geography, and early in July he conducted a conference on Geography in the summer school connected with the University of Pennsylvania.

In the vacation, two courses on Geography were given by Professor Davis in the Harvard Summer School : a first course, on Elementary Physiography, in which he was assisted by Messrs. W. H. Snyder, Master in Science, Worcester Academy, and M. W. Wright, of the College class of '97 ; and a second course on the Physiography of the United States, in which he was assisted by Mr. J. M. Boutwell, '97· As in 1896, the time and effort given to summer teaching are fully repaid by the interest thus aroused among teachers in secondary schools. It is not too much to say that a greater effect is now produced on educational methods in geography through six weeks' work with actual teachers in the summer school than through the whole college year with undergraduates and graduates.

EXCURSIONS AND CONFERENCES.

The following excursions were offered in 1896-97, — several of them in co-operation with geologists from other New England colleges : —

Nahant, Mass.; Professor Shaler.
New Haven, Conn.; Professor Davis.
Hoosac Mountain, Mass.; Professor Wolff.
Coastal Plain of Southern Maine ; Professor Davis.
Barrington Sandplain, R. I.; Mr. J. B. Woodworth.
Ipswich Dunes, Mass. ; Mr. J. H. Sears, of Salem.
Meriden, Conn. ; Professor Davis.
Franklin Furnace, N. J. ; Professor Wolff.
Northampton, Mass. ; Professor B. K. Emerson, of Amherst College.
The Narragansett Basin, R. I. ; Mr. J. B. Woodworth.

The following subjects were discussed at the Geological Conference : —

The Eruptive Rocks of Sussex County, N. J.; Professor Wolff.
The excursion to the Coastal Plain of Southwestern Maine; Professor Davis.
The excursion to Hoosac Mountain (illustrated by stereopticon) ; Professor Wolff.
Some features of the Cornwallis Valley, N. S. ; Mr. V. F. Marsters.
Exhibition of a new Goniometer ; Dr. Charles Palache.
Note on the Hurricane of October 10-14 ; Mr. R. DeC. Ward.
An Instrument for inclining a Preparation in the Microscope; Mr. T. A. Jaggar.
The Geology of Nahant ; Professor Shaler.
The Tourmalines of Mt. Mica, Maine ; Dr. Charles Palache.
A remarkable Joint Specimen from Somerville, Mass.; Mr. J. B. Woodworth.
Material illustrating the Appendages of Trilobites ; Dr. R. T. Jackson.
Magnetic Observations in Geological Mapping; Professor Smyth.
The Structure and Formation of Agates (illustrated by projection apparatus) ; Dr. W. S. Bigelow.
Geological History of the Cape Cod District; Professor Shaler.
The Deflective Force of the Earth's Rotation ; Professor Davis.
Some Phenomena of Steel; Mr. R. J: Forsythe.
The Elæolite Syenite of the Serra Monchique in Portugal; Dr. F. L. Ransome.

The Influence of Initial Fracture and Rate of Compression in Mountain-building (illustrated by models); Mr. T. A. Jaggar.

The Elevated Reef of Florida; Mr. J. E. Woodman.

The Grain of Rocks; Dr. A. C. Lane.

A Proposed Classification in Anthropo-climatology; Mr. R. DeC. Ward.

The Wamsutta Group in the Narragansett Basin; Messrs. H. F. Kendall and G. Buckman.

The Dikes of the Richmond Basin; Mr. J. B. Woodworth.

The Anticlinal and Synclinal Ridges of Pennsylvania; Mr. A. P. Chittenden.

The Gold District of Clay County, Ala.; Professor Shaler.

Notes on the Origin of Petroleum; Mr. G. B. Richardson.

A Geographical Model; Mr. G. C. Curtis.

The Critical Temperatures of Steel; Mr. R. J. Forsythe.

Sandplain Growth in relation to Water Level; Mr. T. A. Jaggar.

The Turkey Branch Section of the Newark Rocks in the Richmond Basin; Mr. J. B. Woodworth.

Post-glacial History of the Connecticut River at Turner's Falls; Mr. M. S. W. Jefferson.

The Geological Aspects of the Narrative of Nansen's last Voyage; Professor Shaler.

Model of a Fjorded Coast; Mr. G. C. Curtis.

Glacial Phenomena, Past and Present, in Greenland, Baffin Land, and Labrador; Professor G. H. Barton.

Dr. Archibald Bruce, Pioneer in American Mineralogy; Professor Wolff.

Natural Coke from the Richmond Basin; Mr. G. B. Richardson.

Recent Studies on the Glacial Great Lakes; Professor Davis.

Greenland, the Arctic Island Continent (illustrated by stereopticon); Civil Engineer R. E. Peary, U. S. Navy.

A Proposed Scientific Trip to South America; Mr. R. DeC. Ward.

The Crystallization of Calcite; Dr. Charles Palache.

The Inclusion-bearing Basalts of the Boston Basin; Mr. T. A. Jaggar.

The Lewis and Clarke Expedition; Professor Wolff.

REPORT ON COURSES IN MINING GEOLOGY.

By Assistant Professor H. L. Smyth.

DURING the past year the course in Mining Geology (Geology 10) was given in the Mineralogical Section of the University Museum, continuing the arrangement of the preceding two years. It is expected that this course will eventually find permanent quarters in the Cary Building.

The lamented death of Professor Whitney in the summer of 1896 made necessary a rearrangement of the courses in Economic Geology. Geology 18 became a half-course in the first half-year, instead of a full course, and was devoted to the consideration of the non-metalliferous minerals. Professor Shaler undertook the greater part of the work of this course, Mr. Smyth dealing only with sulphur and the salts. It is proposed to continue. this arrangement for the coming year. Professor Whitney's course in the Metals and Metalliferous Ores is represented by the parallel course Geology 10.

The collections in Economic Geology have received important accessions during the year from Butte, Cripple Creek, Mercur, Leadville, etc. Mr. Henning Jennings of Johannisberg has contributed an interesting and valuable collection of ores from the Witwaters Rand district in South Africa.

During the year much time was spent in preparing for publication the results of geological field work done in the Upper Peninsula of Michigan in 1891 and 1892. While the work itself was a private enterprise, an arrangement has been made whereby the results are to be published under the auspices of the Lake Superior Division of the United States Geological Survey. One instalment of the final paper is mentioned in the list of publications which follows.

PUBLICATIONS BY OFFICERS AND STUDENTS OF THE DEPARTMENT OF GEOLOGY AND GEOGRAPHY SINCE THE LAST REPORT.

By N. S. Shaler : —

1. The Glacial Brick Clays of Rhode Island and Southeastern Massachusetts. (With J. B. Woodworth and C. F. Marbut.) 17th Annual Report of the Director, U. S. Geological Survey, Part L, 1896, pp. 957–974, 999–1004.

2. Abstract of Administrative Report, for year 1895–96. 17th Annual Report of the Director, U. S. Geological Survey, Part I., 1896, p. 18.

3. Fourth Annual Report Massachusetts Highway Commission. (With Thos. C. Mendenhall and W. E. McClintock.)

4. Nansen's Heroic Journey. Atlantic Monthly, May, 1897, Vol. LXXIX. pp. 610–617.

By W. M. Davis : —

1. The State Map of New York as an Aid to the Study of Geography. University State of New York, Examination Bulletin No. 11, Nov., 1896, pp. 503–526.

2. The State Map of Massachusetts as an Aid to the Study of Geography in Grammar and High Schools. Boston, 1897.

3. The Harvard Geographical Models, with a Note on the Construction of the Models by G. C. Curtis. Proc. Boston Soc. Nat. Hist., Vol. XXVIII., 1897, pp. 85–110.

4. The Present Trend of Geography. Bull. University of the State of New York, 1897.

5. Current Notes on Physiography. Science (through the year).

6. Outline of Requirements in Physiography, 1897. Harvard University.

7. Outline of Requirements in Meteorology (with R. DeC. Ward), 1897. Harvard University, pp. 16.

8. Home Geography. Jour. School Geography, I., 1897, pp. 2–7. Translated in Zeitschr. f. Schulgeogr., XVIII., 1897, pp. 225–229.

9. The Use of Periodicals. Ibid., I., 1897, pp. 81–85.

10. The Temperate Zones. Ibid., I., 1897, pp. 139–143.

11. Topographic Maps of the United States. Ibid., I., 1807, pp. 200–204.

12. Notices of Geographical Publications relating to the United States (with J. M. Boutwell). Annales de Géogr., Bibliogr. de Géogr., Paris, 1897.

By H. L. Smyth : —

Magnetic Observations in Geological Mapping. Trans. Amer. Inst. M. E., XXVI., 1897.

By R. DeC. Ward : —

1. Outline of Requirements in Meteorology. (With W. M. Davis.) 1897, Harvard University, pp. 16.
2. Meteorological Observations in Schools. Jour. School Geography, Feb., 1897.
3. Current Notes on Meteorology. Science (through the year).

By J. B. Woodworth : —

1. The Retreat of the Ice-sheet in the Narragansett Bay Region. The Amer. Geol., Vol. XVIII., 1896, pp. 150–168, Map, Pl. VI.
2. The Ice-sheet in Glacial Narragansett Bay. Ibid., pp. 391, 392.
3. Charles Thomas Jackson. Ibid., Vol. XX., 1897, pp. 69–110. Portrait, Pl. IV. Bibliography, pp. 87–110.
4. On the Fracture System of Joints, with Remarks on certain great Fractures. Proc. Boston Soc. Nat. Hist., Vol. XXVII., 1896, pp. 169–183. 5 plates.
5. The Queen's River Moraine in Rhode Island. The Journ. Geol. (Chicago), Vol. IV., 1896, pp. 691–703. 7 figs. (With C. F. Marbut.)
6. Gibbers. Science, N. S., Vol. V., 1897, pp. 476, 477.
7. Unconformities of Martha's Vineyard and Block Island. Bull. Geol. Soc. Am., Vol. VIII., 1897, pp. 197–212. 1 map and 4 figs.
Abstract in the Journ. Geol. (Chicago), Vol. V., 1897, pp. 96, 97. Also Science, Vol. V., 1897, pp. 86, 87.
8. The Glacial Brick-clays of Rhode Island and Southeastern Massachusetts, by N. S. Shaler, J. B. Woodworth, and C. F. Marbut. Chap. II. Geology and Geography of the Clays. 17th Annual Report of the Director of the U. S. Geol. Survey, Pt. I., 1896, pp. 975–988. 1 map and figures.
9. The Clays about Boston (with C. F. Marbut). Ibid., Chap. III. pp. 989–998.
10. [Itinerary of a course of field work in Southeastern New England.] The Summer School. Harvard University, 1897. Pamphlet, pp. 38–44. Bibliography, pp. 40–44.
11. Homology of Joints and artificial Fractures. Abstract in the Journ. Geol. (Chicago), Vol. V., 1897, pp. 97, 98. Also in Science, Vol. V., 1897, p. 84.
12. Review of Rocks, Rock-weathering, and Soils, by George P. Merrill. Science, Vol. V., 1897, pp. 995–997.

By T. A. Jaggar : —

1. A Simple Instrument for inclining a Preparation in the Microscope. Am. Journ. of Sci., Vol. III. p. 129.

2. Ein Mikrosklerometer zur Härtebestimmung. Groth's Zeitschrift für Krystallographie, Munich. (In press.)

3. Edited Proceedings of Geological Conference of Harvard University, in Science, Vol. IV. No. 101.

By R. A. Daly (omitted from previous Report) : —

The Quartz-porphyry and associated Rocks of Pequawket Mountain, N. H. Science, Vol. III., 1896, p. 752.

By J. E. Woodman : —

[Review of the Elevated Reef of Florida. By Alexander Agassiz. With Notes on the Geology of Southern Florida. By Leon S. Griswold.] The Jour. of Geol., Vol. V., 1897, pp. 312, 313.

By A. P. Chittenden : —

Mountain Structure of Pennsylvania. Bull. Amer. Geogr. Soc., Vol. XXIX. No. 2, 1897, pp. 175–180.

REPORT ON THE INSTRUCTION IN ZOÖLOGY.

By Professor E. L. Mark.

ACCORDING to the proposal announced in my last Report, the courses in Zoölogy, till then designated as Zoölogy 6 and Zoölogy 7^1, were so expanded as to constitute the equivalent of three full courses, one course and a half being given in alternate years. The courses for the Academic year 1896–97 are designated as Courses 11 and 16^1; those for the coming year will be 10 and 15^1. Otherwise there was no considerable change in the work of the Department.

The number of students from the various schools and classes in each of the courses in Zoölogy for the past year is given, as usual, in the accompanying table.

Courses, 1896–97.	Grad.	Sen.	Jun.	Soph.	Fresh.	Spec.	°Sci.	Total.
Zoölogy 1 . . .		12	20	28	26	8	37	131
" 2 . . .	3	5	6	9	2	3	17	45
" 3 . . .	5	8	10	2			14	39
" 4 . . .	2	4	2				5	13
" 5 . . .	2	4	2				4	12
" 11 . . .	6	2					2	10
" 16 . . .	7	8	2	1			4	22
" 20a . . .	10						1	11
Totals . . .	35	43	42	40	28	11	84	283

Two large rooms on the second floor of the Museum, vacated by Dr. Wolff at the beginning of the Academic year, were assigned by the Curator to the Department of Zoölogy. One of these, the east room (No. 5), was converted into a lecture room ⁄and a laboratory for students engaged in research, being fitted up with tables and the necessary appliances. This furnished accommodations for the overflow from room No. 4, which had been temporarily provided for in the previous year by the liberality of the late Professor Whitney, who had surrendered for the year 1895–96 his lecture room on the first floor to the Department of Zoölogy for this purpose.

The other room, the west one (No. 6), was assigned as a private laboratory to Doctors Davenport, Parker, Woodworth, and Mayer. Zoölogy 1 was conducted by Dr. Davenport, substantially as last year. The Chief Assistant was Mr. H. R. Linville, the same as in the preceding year. Messrs. F. C. Lucas, W. J. Moenkhaus, S. R. Williams, and A. S. Hanna were Sub-Assistants.

In Zoölogy 2 the Department was also fortunate enough to have the services as Chief Assistant of the same person who had been Chief Assistant in the preceding year, Mr. J. I. Hamaker. The Sub-Assistant was Mr. R. W. Hall. The course was conducted by Dr. Parker without essential change from the plan of previous years.

A considerable increase in the number of students taking Zoölogy 3 caused the laboratory facilities to be taxed to their utmost. Any further increase in numbers would have to. be met by increasing the number of days on which laboratory work might be done, and probably also by restricting the special topic work to those best qualified to profit by it. The course was conducted by Dr. Parker, who had as Assistants Messrs. J. H.' Hathaway and R. W. Hall. The paper by Mr. Waite prepared in this course last year is now in press.

The lectures in Zoölogy 4 and 5 were given in the new room on the second floor; the laboratory work was done as usual in room No. 2 on the fourth floor. Dr. Woodworth conducted the laboratory work in both these courses, and gave a portion of the lectures in Course 4. The ground covered in the lectures and the material used in the laboratory work were substantially the same as in previous years. The courses were given as in previous years by Drs. Mark and Woodworth.

In Zoölogy 11, by Dr. Davenport, there were lectures throughout the year on phylogenetic problems. A separate topic was assigned to each of the ten students for special study. The results of some of these studies, though not yet in final shape, will be ready for publication before long. The laboratory work was mostly done in Room 5, Floor 2, the room assigned to students in Zoölogy 20a. This arrangement, so far as concerns the supervision of the work in this course, was an improvement on that of the previous year; but it is always undesirable to have the same table used for two kinds of work under the supervision of different instructors. But besides this, there is urgent need of rooms properly equipped for chemical, electrical, thermic, and photic work, which cannot be attempted under present conditions with any likelihood of success. Since my last Report the following " Contributions " embodying work done in connection with this course have been published : Nos. LXXII., LXXIV., and LXXIX. of the list embraced in this Report.

Zoölogy 16, by Dr. Parker, was given this year in accordance with the plan announced last year. After a short introduction to the study of the nervous system, the remaining lectures in the course were devoted to an extended consideration of the anatomy and physiology of the central nervous organs, and the terminal organs of efferent nerves. The experiment was tried of requiring each student to prepare a short paper on some topic connected with the subject matter of the lectures. This exercise, though stimulating to the student, can, of course, never form a satisfactory substitute for laboratory work. There were in regular attendance on the lectures four students who were not enrolled.

The number of students in Zoölogy 20a was not quite as large as in the previous year, but with the research students in Radcliffe College absorbed the most of the time of the instructor left from the work of Zoölogy 4 and 5. The " Contributions " written in this course, which have been completed and published since my last Report, are : Nos. LXX., LXXI., LXXVII., and LXXXI.; those which are " in press " are two by Porter, and one each by Neal, Lewis, Hamaker, and Linville.

At the last Commencement, the degree of Doctor of Science in Zoölogy was conferred upon Mr. Alfred Goldsborough Mayer, whose thesis was completed and published in the spring of 1896, and who was allowed, for reasons stated in my last Report, to come up for his examination in the autumn of 1896 ; also the degree of Doctor of Philosophy upon two candidates in Zoölogy, Mr. John Irvin Hamaker and Mr. Henry Richardson Linville. The titles of their theses appear in the Contributions now " in press."

Dr. H. S. Jennings has resigned the travelling Parker Fellowship, and returned to America. He expects to give his time in future to teaching and research. As the result of his studies in Jena during the winter, he has published in the Journal of Physiology a paper entitled, " Studies on Reactions to Stimuli in Unicellular Organisms. I. Reactions to Chemical, Osmotic, and Mechanical Stimuli in the Ciliate Infusoria."

The degree of A. M. was conferred on three students whose work was wholly or almost wholly in Zoölogy. The continued generosity of the Curator of the Museum and the Corporation has permitted the publication in the Museum Bulletin of the greater number of the following Contributions from the Zoölogical Laboratory, all of which have appeared since my last Report: —

LXX. JENNINGS, H. S. — The Early Development of Asplanchna Herrickii de Guerne. A Contribution to Developmental Mechanics. Bull. Mus. Comp. Zoöl., Vol. XXX. No. 1, pp. 1–118. 10 Pls. October, 1896.

LXXI. NEAL, H. V. — A Summary of Studies on the Segmentation of the Nervous System in Squalus acanthias. A Preliminary Notice. Anat. Anzeiger, Bd. XII. No. 17, pp. 377–391. 6 Figs. October 20, 1896.

LXXII. DAVENPORT, C. B., AND CANNON, W. B. — On the Determination of the Direction and Rate of Movement of Organisms by Light. Jour. of Physiol., Vol. XXXI. No. 1, pp. 27–32. 1 Fig. February 5, 1897.

LXXIII. DAVENPORT, C. B., AND BULLARD, C. — Studies in Morphogenesis, VI. A Contribution to the Quantitative Study of Correlated Variation and the Comparative Variability of the Sexes. Proc. Amer. Acad., Vol. XXXII. No. 4, pp. 87–97. December, 1896.

LXXIV. MAYER, A. G. — On the Color and Color-Patterns of Moths and Butterflies. Bull. Mus. Comp. Zoöl., Vol. XXX. No. 4, pp. 167–256. 10 Pls. Feb. [Mar.], 1897. Also Proc. Bost. Soc. Nat. Hist., Vol. XXVII. No. 14, pp. 243–330. 10 Pls. March, 1897.

LXXV. PARKER, G. H. — The Mesenteries and Siphonoglyphs in Metridium marginatum Milne-Edwards. Bull. Mus. Comp. Zoöl., Vol. XXX. No. 5, pp. 257–272. 1 Pl. March, 1897.

LXXVI. PARKER, G. H. — Photomechanical Changes in the Retinal Pigment Cells of Palæmonetes, and their Relation to the Central Nervous System. Bull. Mus. Comp. Zoöl., Vol. XXX. No. 6, pp. 273–300. 1 Pl. April, 1897.

LXXVII. BUNKER, F. S. — On the Structure of the Sensory Organs of the Lateral Line of Ameiurus nebulosus Le Sueur. Anat. Anzeiger, Bd. XIII. No. 8 u. 9, pp. 256–260. March 3, 1897.

LXXVIII. WOODWORTH, W. McM. — On a Method of Graphic Reconstruction from Serial Sections. Zeitschr. f. wiss. Mikr., Bd. XIV. No. 1, pp. 15–18. July, 1897.

LXXIX. BREWSTER, E. T. — A Measure of Variability, and the Relation of Individual Variations to Specific Differences. Proc. Amer. Acad., Vol. XXXII. No. 15, pp. 269–279. May, 1897.

LXXX. DAVENPORT, C. B. — The Rôle of Water in Growth. Proc. Bost. Soc. Nat. Hist., Vol. XXVIII. No. 3, pp. 73–84. June, 1897.

LXXXI. LEWIS, MARGARET. — Clymene producta, sp. n. Proc. Bost. Soc. Nat. Hist., Vol. XXVIII. No. 5, pp. 111–117. 2 Pls. August, 1897.

In Press.

PORTER, J. F. — Two new Gregarinida. Jour. of Morphol., Vol. XIV. No. 1, pp. 1–20. 3 Pls. 1897.

WOODWORTH, W. McM. — Contributions to the Morphology of the Turbellaria. II. On some Turbellaria from Illinois. Bull. Mus. Comp. Zoöl., Vol. XXXI. No. 1, pp. 1–16. 1 Pl. October, 1897.

PORTER, J. F. — Trichonympha, and other Parasites of Termes flavipes. Bull. Mus. Comp. Zoöl., Vol. XXXI. No. 3, pp. 45–68. 6 Pls. October, 1897.

WAITE, F. C. — Variations in the Brachial and Lumbo-Sacral Plexi of Necturus maculosus Rafinesque. Bull. Mus. Comp. Zoöl., Vol. XXXI. No. 4, pp. 69–92. 2 Pls. November, 1897.

LEWIS, MARGARET. — Studies on the Central and Peripheral Nervous System of Two Polychæte Annelids. Proc. Amer. Acad. 8 Pls.

DAVENPORT, C. B., AND PERKINS, HELEN. — A Contribution to the Study of Geotaxis in the Higher Animals. Jour. of Physiol., Vol. XXII. Nos. 1 and 2, pp. 99–110. Sept. 1, 1897.

NEAL, H. V. — The Segmentation of the Nervous System in Squalus acanthias. Bull. Mus. Comp. Zoöl., Vol. XXXI. No. 5. 9 Pls.

HAMAKER, J. I. — The Nervous System of Nereis virens Sars. A Study in Comparative Neurology. Bull. Mus. Comp. Zoöl., Vol. XXXI. No. 6. 5 Pls.

LINVILLE, H. R. — Maturation and Fertilization in Pulmonate Gasteropods.

During the Academic year 1896–97 the Division of Natural History under the Faculty of Arts and Sciences was split into two divisions, one of which, Biology, embraces the two Departments of Botany and Zoölogy. Dr. Farlow of the Botanical Department has been made Chairman, and Dr. Davenport has been chosen Secretary of this Division.

Hereafter Dr. R. T. Jackson is to give in the Zoölogical Department a course in Palæozoölogy under the title, "Fossil Invertebrates, — Lectures and Laboratory Work." This course is to run through the whole year, and is to be designated Zoölogy 9 ; it will be somewhat similar to the course Geology 13 of previous years, this course being discontinued.

It is with regret that I record the resignation of Dr. W. McM. Woodworth from the teaching force of the Department, to take effect at the beginning of the next Academic year. I wish to express the feeling of loss which we as a Department experience in the transference of Dr. Woodworth's energies from the College to the Museum, which is hereafter to receive all his attention, and further, to express the hope that at some time in the future a portion of his time may be again given to the work of instruction.

To provide for the work in teaching hitherto carried on by Dr. Woodworth, and at the same time to relieve Dr. Parker of a portion of his duties in instruction, Dr. William E. Castle has been appointed Instructor in Anatomy and Embryology. Besides assisting in the courses in Microscopical Anatomy and Embryology of Vertebrates (Zoölogy 4 and 5), he will have charge of Zoölogy 2.

Dr. Davenport, in addition to the work which he has done in connection with the courses under his charge and the papers produced in connection with them, has published Part I. of his work on "Experimental Morphology." This part deals with "Effect of Chemical and Physical Agents on Protoplasm," and is a book of nearly 300 pages, issued by the Macmillan Company, New York, 1897. Part II. of this work is also nearly completed. He has also published an article "On the Rôle of Water in Growth," as Contribution No. LXXX., and, in collaboration with Mr. C. Bullard, Contribution No. LXXIII. He has besides written for "Science" a review of the works of O. Hertwig and E. B. Wilson on "The Cell," and several reviews for "L'Année biologique," Tom. I., as well as an article on "College Admission Requirements" for the "Harvard Graduates' Magazine," December, 1896.

Dr. Parker has published two interesting illustrated papers : one on "The Mesenteries and Siphonoglyphs in Metridium," the other on "Photomechanical Changes in the Retinal Pigment Cells of Palæmonetes," etc., as Contributions LXXV. and LXXVI.

The paper on "Some Variations in the Genus Eucope," by the Curator and Dr. Woodworth, has been published since my last Report, and Dr. Woodworth has also published an article "On a

Method of Graphic Reconstruction from Serial Sections," Contribution No. LXXVIII. Another article by him on the Turbellaria of Illinois is now in the hands of the printer.

Early in the year the Department collections were enriched by a valuable and expensive series of Thiersch's transparent injection preparations, presented by Mr. B. S. Oppenheimer.

Near the middle of the College year the Zoölogical Club changed the time of its meetings from the evening to half-past four in the afternoon. From that time forward the meetings were held every week, instead of every two weeks as in previous years. Soon afterwards the advanced students in Zoölogy in Radcliffe College were invited to attend and participate in the discussions of the Club. The invitation was generally accepted. The meetings were well attended and the discussions profitable.

The number of students enrolled in the Zoölogical Courses in Radcliffe College was as follows: —

Zoölogy	1	2	3	4	5	15	20a
No. of Students	14	9	4	2	2	5	6

REPORT ON THE MAMMALS AND BIRDS.

By WILLIAM BREWSTER.

THE past year has been singularly uneventful as far as the present department is concerned. Practically no changes have been made in the arrangements of the collections, and the only acquirements are the following

By gift. From William Brewster, a Mole (*Parascalops breweri*) from Lake Umbagog, Maine ; two skins of Xantus's Jay (*Aphelocoma c. hypoleuca*), taken at La Paz, Lower California, by M. A. Frazer, and four skins of the Florida Crow (*Corvus a. floridanus*), taken at Fort Myers, Florida, by W. E. D. Scott. From Mrs. J. J. Glesner, a double nest of a Vireo (apparently *V. olivaceus*). Twenty-three skins of Mammals from Borneo and Great Natuna Island, and nineteen skins of birds from Borneo and Celebes, collected by E. and C. Hose, were presented by Dr. W. H. Furness through Professor Jayne.

During the past winter Mr. G. S. Miller, Jr., has made extensive use of the Museum material in connection with the study and determination of a collection of Mammals and Birds obtained by him in the region north of Lake Superior in the summer of 1896. Lieut. W. Robinson has also consulted the collections on several occasions, and Mr. Freeze of the Washington Grammar School has been supplied with bird skins which he has used for purposes of instruction in the school. These specimens have been duly returned. It is to be regretted that assistance of this kind cannot be more freely and generally given, but for the reason explained by Mr. Agassiz in his Report for 1890 and 1891 (pp. 8 and 9), it is impracticable to do this to any considerable extent.

The general condition of the collections is most satisfactory. Insect pests appear to have been wholly exterminated. At least, during the past year no signs of their presence have been detected.

The Assistant in this department has published the following papers and notes in " The Auk."

Occurrence of the Wood Ibis (*Tantalus loculator*) in Bristol County, Massachusetts.

On the Nomenclature of certain Forms of the Downy Woodpecker (*Dryobates pubescens*).

The Lesser Snow Goose in New England.

The Bahaman Swallow in Florida.

REPORT ON THE REPTILES AND FISHES.

By SAMUEL GARMAN.

MUCH the largest addition to these collections was obtained in exchange from Dr. Fernand Lataste. It was composed of desirable representatives of the faunas of Chili and of Algeria, Reptiles, Batrachians, and Fishes. Mr. W. H. Phelps donated the fine collection of Reptiles and Batrachians secured by him in Venezuela to these departments, after making a thorough study of it in connection with the Museum's material. The "Great Barrier Reef Expedition" of 1896 supplied an excellent series of Australian desiderata, collected by Messrs. Woodworth, Mayer, and Olive. Outram Bangs, Esq., added quite a number of species to his contributions from Florida. Accessions from various localities have also been received from Professor G. H. Parker, Dr. L. C. Jones, and Messrs. I. T. Jones, Roswell H. Johnson, Herbert W. Taylor, C. M. F. Flagg, and Lawrence Brooks. All receipts were in good condition.

Few shipments have been made. Besides what was furnished to the students in Zoölogy, a small lot of fishes went to the Laboratory of Indiana University. The material collected by Professor C. C. Nutting on his Expedition to the Bahamas, Cuba, and Florida Keys, for the University of Iowa, was made the basis of a report, and was returned to the University. The report as published is entitled "Report on the Fishes collected by the Bahama Expedition of the State University of Iowa, under Professor C. C. Nutting, in 1893," and appeared in the Bulletin of the Laboratory of Natural Sciences of the Iowa University, in 1896, and separately as a reprint.

Aside from the routine demands of the Exhibition series, and of the storage collections, the greater portion of the labor has been devoted to a continuation of the studies in deep-sea ichthyology, identification, dissection, drawing, all being more or less directly connected with that work, now approaching completion.

Of the general condition in the rooms occupied by the Fishes and Reptiles it may be said that the amount of loss, on account of decay, insect ravages, discoloration, evaporation, or breakage, is the smallest yet reported.

REPORT ON THE ENTOMOLOGICAL DEPARTMENT.

By Samuel Henshaw.

For acceptable additions to the collections, the Department is indebted to Miss Isabel Johnson, Messrs. A. L. Babcock, Outram Bangs, C. F. Batchelder, Frederick Blanchard, Charles Bullard, H. K. Burrison, P. P. Calvert, J. H. Emerton, W. G. Farlow, Walter Faxon, W. F. Fiske, J. W. Folsom, H. G. Gallagher, G. L. Goodale, Roland Hayward, Ralph Hoffmann, G. H. Horn, J. G. Jack, R. T. Jackson, A. G. Mayer, G. S. Miller, Jr., A.-P. Morse, A. S. Packard, Wirt Robinson, S. H. Scudder, F. A. Sherriff, Roland Thaxter, C. M. Weed, W. L. Wilder, J. B. Woodworth, W. McM. Woodworth, and C. E. Worthington.

The Assistant has added several hundred specimens collected in Massachusetts and Southern New Hampshire. Many students and specialists have worked upon the collections during the past year.

The condition of the collections is highly satisfactory; at the last thorough examination, just completed, not a single case of injury from Anthreni or other destructive insects was discovered.

A revisional rearrangement of the Euchromiidæ, Notodontidæ, Saturniidæ, and Thyatiridæ of the Lepidoptera Heterocera, and of the Scutelleridæ of the Hemiptera Heteroptera, has been completed. Several genera of the Lepidoptera Rhopalocera have also been rearranged, and some additional progress made with portions of the Carabidæ, Scarabæidæ, and Tenebrionidæ of the Coleoptera. The rearrangement of the large series of Cynipidous galls has been begun, but is not completed.

In the Leconte collection of Coleoptera the final rearrangement of the Dascyllidæ, Rhipiceridæ, Elateridæ, Throscidæ, Buprestidæ, Lampyridæ, Malachidæ, Cleridæ, Ptinidæ, Cupesidæ, Lymexylidæ, Lucanidæ, Scarabæidæ, Spondylidæ, and Cerambycidæ has been completed.

Nine large boxes of galls have been prepared for exhibition in the Botanical Section of the Museum. This series includes some of the more important and commoner North American and European galls made by insects and mites; brief labels describe these galls, and in a few cases the architects of the galls are shown.

REPORT ON THE CRUSTACEA AND MOLLUSCA.

By WALTER FAXON.

GIFTS of Crustacea and Mollusca have been received during the past year from Messrs. A. Agassiz, H. Ayers, O. Bangs, J. H. Blake, H. Garman, W. A. Hickman, R. T. Jackson, A. M. Norman, A. Ortmann, and W. McM. Woodworth. Of these the most valuable is a lot of Crustacea, comprising twenty-two species from Greenland and Davis Straits, — the gift of the Rev. A. M. Norman.

In the winter of 1893–94, I undertook, with Miss Parker's assistance, the systematic arrangement of the large collection of Molluscan shells stored in two rooms on the fifth floor of the Museum. A brief statement of the then condition of the collection, together with the system to be observed in its revision, was made in my Report for 1893–94. This work was brought to a finish during the spring of the present year. The shells are now not only easily accessible, but also (as I hope) in a state of permanent safety. The collection as now arranged is contained in 1,730 wooden drawers or trays (26½ × 17 in., inside measurement). Of these (to specify some of the larger divisions) the Muricidæ occupy 39 trays, the Volutidæ 44, the Conidæ 39, the Strombidæ 39, the Cypræidæ 48, the Melaniidæ 54, the Trochidæ 50, the Helicidæ 314, the Tellinidæ 35, the Veneridæ 47; the Unionidæ 271. In this collection are included the types of the shells described by J. G. Anthony and by Temple Prime; in many groups, moreover, the identifications were made by Mr. Anthony through a direct collation with the original types, so that the specimens have come to have a value second only to types.

The alcoholic collection of Mollusks, stored in the basement of the building, fills 95 trays. Here is found most of the deep-sea material from the "Blake" and "Albatross" dredgings, — material elaborated by Messrs. W. H. Dall and A. E. Verrill.

These collections, together with the extensive suites of mounted specimens in the Exhibition Rooms, make up the Molluscan wealth of the Museum.

REPORT ON THE VERMES.

By W. McM. Woodworth.

DURING the past year the entire collection of Annelids has been catalogued and arranged systematically, and considerable progress has been made in cataloguing and arranging the other groups. The chief additions to the collections are a fine series of New Zealand and Australian Land Planarians received from Mr. Arthur Dendy, a collection of British Turbellaria from Mr. A. Lyster Jameson, a collection of fresh-water Planarians from Professor Paul Hallez, and one of Nemerteans from Dr. T. H. Montgomery. Thanks are also due to Professor J. S. Kingsley for contributions to the collections.

The Museum Gordiidæ were sent to Dr. T. H. Montgomery, and have been returned by him with a report based upon the collection. The Arenicolidæ have been forwarded to Mr. F. W. Gamble, of Queen's College, Manchester.

The United States National Museum collection of Nemerteans has been lent to the Assistant. This supplemented by the Museum material forms a superb collection for the study of the representatives of this group from the Atlantic and Pacific coasts.

The Assistant has published the following papers during the past year : —

Notes on Turbellaria. Am. Naturalist, Vol. XXX., 1896.

On the Occurrence of Filaroides mustelarum in American Skunks. Am. Naturalist, Vol. XXXI., 1897.

The Cambridge Natural History (a review). Science, N. S., Vol. V. No. 129, 1897.

On a Method of Graphic Reconstruction from Serial Sections. Zeitschr. f. wiss. Mikroskopie, Bd. XIV., 1897.

Contributions to the Morphology of the Turbellaria. II. On some Turbellaria from Illinois. Bull. Mus. Comp. Zoöl., Vol. XXXI. No. 1. 1897.

A report on the Planarians collected by the Barrier Reef Expedition is nearly ready for the printer, and good progress has been made with the " Albatross " Nemerteans.

REPORT ON THE ECHINODERMS, POLYPS, ETC.

By Alfred G. Mayer.

The time of the Assistant has been mainly devoted to a general inspection and revision of the collection.

Many of the *ink written* labels of the alcoholic specimens had faded to such an extent as to be almost illegible. This was especially true of the Pourtalès types of Deep-Sea Corals. Several hundred labels were copied and replaced. In only two cases was it found impossible to decipher the original label.

The Assistant has added to the collection about thirty species of Medusæ, preserved in 5% formalin.

These were for the most part obtained at the Newport Laboratory. In addition to the above, about twenty-five species of Hydromedusæ from the Dry Tortugas, most of which are new to science, have been placed in the collection.

It is found that excellent Museum specimens of Medusæ may be made by killing and preserving them in 5% formalin. In many cases the animal is preserved in a perfectly natural attitude, and the gelatinous substance of the bell, etc. remains transparent. The colors of the proboscis, etc., however, usually fade, and the specimens are not suitable for histological work.

The Assistant has published " A New Hypothesis of Seasonal-Dimorphism in Lepidoptera," in Psyche, a Journal of Entomology, May – June, 1897.

REPORT ON THE DEPARTMENT OF VERTEBRATE PALÆONTOLOGY.

By CHARLES R. EASTMAN.

THE most important additions to the collection since the date of the last Report consist of a unique series of Devonian Fishes from Iowa, and a number of choice specimens from the Cleveland Shale of Ohio. Several boxes of material from a newly discovered fishbed in Johnson County, Iowa, were very generously presented by the State Geologist, Professor Samuel Calvin, and arrangements have since been made by which the Museum is enabled to participate in the further exploitation of this interesting deposit. A second instalment of Ohio material, purchased of Dr. William Clark, secured to the Department a valuable lot of specimens ; and the representation of fossil Vertebrates from this State has been still further increased by exchanges, as noted below. It is fortunate that the faunal series should have become thus enriched in a direction wherein there formerly existed a deficiency.

The time of the Assistant has been devoted principally to the care and study of the collections under his charge. The display of specimens in the Systematic Exhibition Rooms has been rearranged, and the selection of fossils for the Palæozoic Room brought to a completion. During the present summer a field trip of a month's duration is contemplated. The success that has attended the operations of professional collectors in working up small but productive fields systematically, instead of skimming over a large area superficially, is sufficient demonstration of the economy and advantage of this method as applied to institutions. Concentration of effort in localities where there is a natural concentration of material, well known examples of which occur in this country, insures much better results than desultory gatherings over a wide district.

Additions to the Collection during the Year.

1896.   Specimens of *Macropetalichthys, Gonatodus*, and other remains from the Corniferous Limestone, near Columbus, Ohio.   Exchange with Dr. Edward Orton, State Geologist.   Received December 23.

1896. Calvin Collection. A large assortment of fossil fish remains, chiefly Dipnoan and Chimæroid, from the so-called State Quarry Bed (presumably Upper Devonian) of Johnson County, Iowa. Presented by Professor Samuel Calvin. Received December 24.

1896. Clark Collection. Second instalment of fossil Fishes from the Cleveland Shale of Northern Ohio, including a figured cranium of *Dinichthys intermedius* and good examples of *Cladodus fyleri*. Purchased of Dr. William Clark, Berea, Ohio. Received December 26.

1897. Several well preserved specimens of *Semionotus* and *Catopterus* from the Trias of the Connecticut Valley; also a small collection of Green River Fishes. Exchange with Boston Society of Natural History. Received January 1.

1897. A set of plaster models from the Oxford Museum, presented through E. R. Lankester, Linacre Professor of Zoölogy. Received January 13.

1897. Casts of Palæozoic Fishes and Amphibians, presented by Professor E. D. Cope. Received January 18.

1897. Cavern bones from New South Wales, collected on the Australian Expedition of 1896. Received January 26.

1897. Vertebræ and portions of jaw belonging to type-specimen of *Baptanodon natans* Marsh. Exchange with Professor A. S. Packard. Received February 1.

1897. Specimen of *Macropetalichthys sullivanti*, showing interior of cranium, etc., from the Corniferous Limestone of Ohio. Exchange with Professor C. H. Hitchcock. Received March 22.

Papers Published during the Year.

Daniel Denison Slade [Biographical Sketch of]. New Eng. Hist. and Gen. Register, Vol. LI. pp. 3–14, January.

On the Characters of Macropetalichthys. Amer. Naturalist, Vol. XXXI. pp. 493–499, June.

On Ctenacanthus Spines from the Keokuk Limestone of Iowa. Amer. Journ. Sci. [4], Vol. IV. pp. 10–13, July.

Tamiobatis vetustus, a new Form of Fossil Skate. Amer. Journ. Sci., [4], Vol. IV. pp. 85–90, August.

On the Occurrence of Fossil Fishes in the Devonian of Iowa. Ann. Rep. Iowa Geological Survey, Vol. VII. pp. 108–116.

On the Relations of certain Plates in the Dinichthyids, with Descriptions of new Species. Bull. Mus. Comp. Zoöl., Vol. XXXI. pp. 19–44.

REPORT ON FOSSIL INVERTEBRATES.

By ALPHEUS HYATT.

THE Ammonitinæ of the Cretaceous have been studied and rearranged through the groups of Pseudoceratites and their immediate allies, including also the Phylloceratidæ and part of Lytoceratidæ. During the summer a number of species of Palæozoic Cephalopods have been selected for exhibition.

The Department is indebted to Dr. R. T. Jackson for revising the collections of Pteropods, Lamellibranchs, Worms, and Bryozoa, rearranging parts, and placing the whole in better condition, and also selecting material suitable for exhibition.

Part of the time of two Assistants has been expended in labelling and piecing together specimens of the Schary and other collections, and also in mounting some fossils for exhibition in the Stratigraphic Collection.

Hon. C. D. Walcott and Hon. Frank Springer have looked over parts of the collections, and selected materials to be sent them for investigation, and the latter has donated a choice collection of Palæozoic Crinoids.

Professor C. E. Beecher has given the Department some rare Devonian Phyllopods, and a specimen of Triarthrus beckii showing the appendages on the ventral side, and also his two beautiful restorations of that species illustrating the final results of his successful researches upon the external anatomy.

A lot of fine Trilobites from the Middle Cambrian of Mt. Stephen, British Columbia, has been presented by Messrs. F. N. Balch and G. L. Paine.

The superb work of Wachsmuth and Springer on "North American Crinoidea Camerata," in three large volumes, with eighty-three plates, noticed elsewhere in the list of the Memoirs of this Museum, has been partly based upon the materials accumulated in this department, and shows the exceptionally rich character of the collection of Crinoids.

REPORT ON THE LIBRARY.

BY MISS F. M. SLACK.

DURING the year ending September 1, 1897, the Library has received 548 volumes, 2,335 parts, and 150 pamphlets.

	VOLUMES.	PARTS.	PAMPHLETS.
Gift	13	60	56
Exchange	135	765	53
Purchase	28	270	0
A. Agassiz	176	1,240	41
Binding Parts	196	0	0
	548	2,335	150

The number of volumes now in the Library (exclusive of pamphlets and the Whitney Library) is 23,292. There are 17,251 pamphlets bound in 2,908 volumes, making the total number of volumes 26,200.

To this should be added the Whitney Library, containing about 5,000 volumes and 1,500 pamphlets, making the total volumes 31,200, and about 1,800 pamphlets not yet arranged by subjects for binding.

[A]

PUBLICATIONS

OF THE

MUSEUM OF COMPARATIVE ZOÖLOGY

FOR THE ACADEMIC YEAR 1896-97.

Of the Bulletin : —

Vol. XXVIII. (Geological Series, Vol. III.)

No. 2. The ELEVATED REEF of FLORIDA. By A. AGASSIZ. With Notes on the GEOLOGY of SOUTHERN FLORIDA. By L. S. GRISWOLD. pp. 36. 26 Plates. October, 1896.

No. 3. Notes on the ARTESIAN WELL sunk at KEY WEST, FLORIDA, in 1895. Based on a Collection made for ALEXANDER AGASSIZ. By E. O. HOVEY. pp. 30. December, 1896.

[Vol. XXVIII. will be continued.]

Vol. XXX. (October, 1896–April, 1897.)

No. 1. The Early DEVELOPMENT of ASPLANCHNA HERRICKII de Guerne; a Contribution to Developmental Mechanics. By H. S. JENNINGS. pp. 118. 10 Plates. October, 1896.

No. 2. Studies from the Newport Marine Laboratory. XL. Some VARIATIONS in the Genus EUCOPE. By A. AGASSIZ and W. McM. WOODWORTH. pp. 32. 9 Plates. November, 1896.

No. 3. Reports on the Results of DREDGING in the "BLAKE." XXXVII. Supplementary Notes on the CRUSTACEA. By W. FAXON. pp. 16. 2 Plates. November, 1896.

No. 4. Contributions from the Zoölogical Laboratory. LXXIV. On the COLOR and COLOR-PATTERNS of MOTHS and BUTTERFLIES. By A. G. MAYER. pp. 90. 10 Plates. February, 1897.

No. 5. Contributions from the Zoölogical Laboratory. LXXV. The MESENTERIES and SIPHONOGLYPHS in METRIDIUM MARGINATUM Milne-Edwards. By G. H. Parker. pp. 16. 1 Plate. March, 1897.

No. 6. Contributions from the Zoölogical Laboratory. LXXVI. Photomechanical CHANGES in the RETINAL PIGMENT CELLS of PALÆMONETES, and their Relation to the Central Nervous System. By G. H. PARKER. pp. 27. 1 Plate. April, 1897.

[Vol. XXX. is complete.]

Of the Memoirs: —

Vol. XIX. (July, 1893–May, 1897.)

No. 2. Reports on the Results of DREDGING in the "BLAKE," 1877–1880. XXXV. Description des CRUSTACÉS de la Famille des GALATHÉIDÉS recueillis pendant l'Expédition. Par A. MILNE-EDWARDS et E. L. BOUVIER. pp. 142. 12 Plates. May, 1897.

[Vol. XIX. is complete.]

Vols. XX., XXI. The NORTH AMERICAN CRINOIDEA CAMERATA. By CHARLES WACHSMUTH and FRANK SPRINGER. 2 Vols. pp. 837, and Atlas of 83 Plates. May, 1897.

[B]

INVESTED FUNDS OF THE MUSEUM.

IN THE HANDS OF THE TREASURER OF HARVARD COLLEGE, SEPT. 1, 1895.

Sturgis-Hooper Fund	$100,000.00
Gray Fund	50,000.00
Agassiz Memorial Fund	297,933.10
Teachers and Pupils Fund	7,594.01
Permanent Fund	117,469.34
Humboldt Fund	7,740.66
Virginia Barret Gibbs Fund	5,000.00
	$585,737.11

The payments on account of the Museum are made by the Bursar of Harvard College, on vouchers approved by the Curator. The accounts are annually examined by a committee of the Overseers. The only funds the income of which is restricted, the Gray and the Humboldt Funds, are annually charged in an analysis of the accounts, with vouchers to the payment of which the income is applicable.

The income of the Gray Fund can be applied to the purchase and maintenance of collections, but not for salaries.

The income of the Virginia Barret Gibbs Scholarship Fund, of the value of $250, is assigned annually with the approval of the Faculty of the Museum, at the recommendation of the Professors of Zoölogy and of Comparative Anatomy in Harvard University, " in supporting or assisting to support one or more students who have shown decided talents in Zoölogy, and preferably in the direction of Marine Zoölogy."

The income of the Humboldt Fund (about $300) can be applied for the benefit of one or more students of Natural History, either at the Museum, the United States Fish Commission Station at Wood's Hole, or elsewhere.

Applications for the tables reserved for advanced students at the Wood's Hole Station should be made to the Director of the Museum before the 1st of May. Applicants should state their qualifications, and indicate the course of study they intend to pursue.

The following Publications of the Museum of Comparative Zoölogy are in preparation : —

Reports on the Results of Dredging Operations in 1877, 1878, 1879, and 1880, in charge of ALEXANDER AGASSIZ, by the U. S. Coast Survey Steamer "Blake," as follows : —

E. EHLERS. The Annelids of the "Blake."
C. HARTLAUB. The Comatulæ of the "Blake," with 15 Plates.
H. LUDWIG. The Genus Pentacrinus.
A. E. VERRILL. The Alcyonaria of the "Blake."

Illustrations of North American MARINE INVERTEBRATES, from Drawings by BURKHARDT, SONREL, and A. AGASSIZ, prepared under the Direction of L. AGASSIZ.

A. AGASSIZ. A Visit to the Great Barrier Reef of Australia.
LOUIS CABOT. Immature State of the Odonata, Part IV.
E. L. MARK. Studies on Lepidosteus, continued.
" On Arachnactis.
R. T. HILL. On the Geology of the Isthmus of Panama.
" On the Geology of Jamaica.
" On the Geology of the Windward Islands.

Contributions from the ZOÖLOGICAL LABORATORY, in charge of Professor E. L. MARK.

Contributions from the GEOLOGICAL LABORATORY, in charge of Professor N. S. SHALER.

Studies from the NEWPORT MARINE LABORATORY, communicated by ALEXANDER AGASSIZ, as follows : —

A. AGASSIZ and A. G. MAYER. The Acalephs of the East Coast of the United States.
" " " On Dactylometra quinquecirra Agass.
AGASSIZ and WHITMAN. Pelagic Fishes. Part II., with 14 Plates.

Reports on the Results of the Expedition of 1891 of the U. S. Fish Commission Steamer "Albatross," Lieutenant Commander Z. L. TANNER, U. S. N., Commanding, in charge of ALEXANDER AGASSIZ, as follows : —

A. AGASSIZ. The Pelagic Fauna.
" The Echini.
" The Panamic Deep-Sea Fauna.
J. E. BENEDICT. The Annelids.
K. BRANDT. The Sagittæ.
" The Thalassicolæ.
C. CHUN. The Siphonophores.
" The Eyes of Deep-Sea Crustacea.
W. H. DALL. The Mollusks.
S. GARMAN. The Fishes.
H. J. HANSEN. The Cirripeds and Isopods.
W. A. HERDMAN. The Ascidians.
S. J. HICKSON. The Antipathids.
W. E. HOYLE. The Cephalopods.
G. VON KOCH. The Deep-Sea Corals.
C. A. KOFOID. Solenogaster.
R. VON LENDENFELD. The Phosphorescent Organs of Fishes.

C. F. LÜTKEN and TH. MORTENSEN. The Ophiuridæ.
O. MAAS. The Acalephs.
E. L. MARK. The Actinarians.
JOHN MURRAY. The Bottom Specimens.
ROBERT RIDGWAY. The Alcoholic Birds.
P. SCHIEMENZ. The Pteropods and Heteropods
W. PERCY SLADEN. The Starfishes.
L. STEJNEGER. The Reptiles.
THEO. STUDER. The Alcyonarians.
M. P. A. TRAÜTSTEDT. The Salpidæ and Doliolidæ.
E. P. VAN DUZEE. The Halobatidæ.
H. B. WARD. The Sipunculids.
H. V. WILSON. The Sponges.
W. McM. WOODWORTH. The Planarians.

PUBLICATIONS

OF THE

MUSEUM OF COMPARATIVE ZOÖLOGY

AT HARVARD COLLEGE.

There have been published of the BULLETINS Vols. I. to XXX.; of the Memoirs, Vols. I. to XVIII. Vols. XXVIII. and XXXI. of the BULLETIN, and Vol. XXIII. of the MEMOIRS, are now in course of publication.

The BULLETIN and MEMOIRS are devoted to the publication of original work by the Professors and Assistants of the Museum, of investigations carried on by students and others in the different Laboratories of Natural History, and of work by specialists based upon the Museum Collections.

The following publications are in preparation : —

Reports on the Results of Dredging Operations from 1877 to 1880, in charge of Alexander Agassiz, by the U. S. Coast Survey Steamer "Blake," Lieut. Commander C. D. Sigsbee, U. S. N., and Commander J. R. Bartlett, U. S. N., Commanding.

Reports on the Results of the Expedition of 1891 of the U. S. Fish Commission Steamer "Albatross," Lieut. Commander Z. L. Tanner, U. S. N., Commanding, in charge of Alexander Agassiz.

Contributions from the Zoölogical Laboratory, in charge of Professor E. L. Mark.

Contributions from the Geological Laboratory, in charge of Professor N. S. Shaler.

Studies from the Newport Marine Laboratory, communicated by Alexander Agassiz.

Subscriptions for the publications of the Museum will be received on the following terms : —

For the BULLETIN, $4.00 per volume, payable in advance.
For the MEMOIRS, $8.00   "   "   "

These publications are issued in numbers at irregular intervals; one volume of the Bulletin (8vo) and half a volume of the Memoirs (4to) usually appear annually. Each number of the Bulletin and of the Memoirs is also sold separately. A price the publications of the Museum will be sent on application to the Director of the Museum of Comparative Zoölogy, Cambridge,

ALEXANDER AGASSIZ, *Director.*